IT'S A FACT! Real-Life Reads

How to Make an

EGYPTIAN MUMMY

by Ruth Owen

Series consultant:

Suzy Gazlay, MA
Recipient, Presidential Award for Excellence in Science Teaching

Ruby Tuesday Books

Published in 2015 by Ruby Tuesday Books Ltd.

Editor: Mark J. Sachner
Designer: Emma Randall
Production: John Lingham

Photo Credits:
Alamy: 6, 11 (bottom); Corbis: 13 (top), 15 (bottom), 17 (bottom); Getty Images: Cover, 29; Istockphoto: 5; Public Domain: 14, 16, 17 (top), 18–19, 20–21, 24–25, 26–27, 28, 31; Science Photo Library: 8–9, 11 (top), 13 (bottom); Shutterstock: 4–5, 7, 10, 12, 22–23, 26 (bottom), 27 (bottom); Superstock: 15 (top).

Library of Congress Control Number: 2014920846

ISBN 978-1-909673-94-6

Printed and published in the United States of America

For further information including rights and permissions requests, please contact our Customer Service Department at 877-337-8577.

Contents

For All Eternity

It is the year 1338 BC. The queen is dead. A slow-moving procession carries her body through the Egyptian desert.

The procession reaches a small building close to the **tombs** of the royal family. This is the workshop of the **embalmers**. Here, a priest and other men are waiting. Using their ancient knowledge and skills, the embalmers will prepare the queen's body for burial.

Ancient Egypt was a civilization that existed from around 3100 BC to 300 BC. All ancient Egyptians wanted their bodies to be **preserved** when they died. Most dead bodies were made into mummies by embalmers. A queen or **pharaoh** received the most special and expensive treatments.

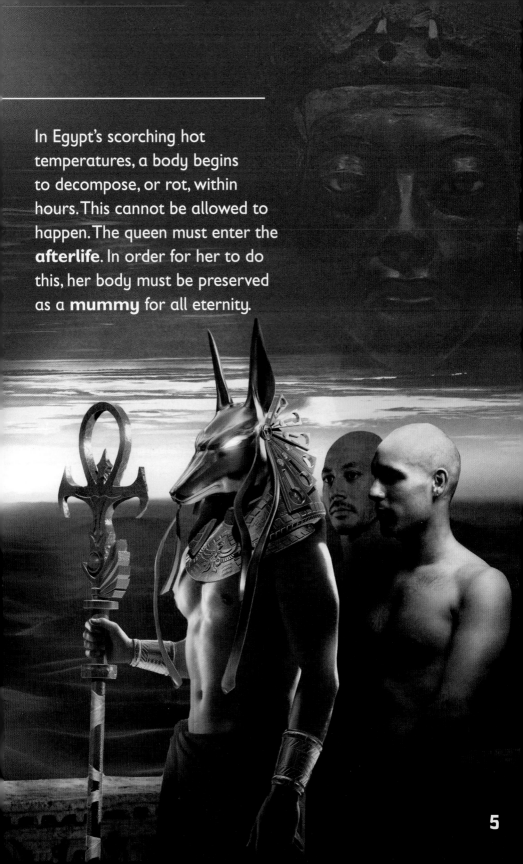

In Egypt's scorching hot temperatures, a body begins to decompose, or rot, within hours. This cannot be allowed to happen. The queen must enter the **afterlife**. In order for her to do this, her body must be preserved as a **mummy** for all eternity.

The Work Begins

When a person died, his or her family brought the body to the embalmers' workshop.

The embalmers began their task by draining any fluids, including blood, from the **corpse**. Next, the body's **organs** had to be removed quickly. This helped stop the body from decomposing.

First, the brain had to be removed without damaging the head. The embalmer took a long, thin, iron tool with a hook on the end. He inserted the tool into the corpse's left nostril. Then the tool was twirled around inside the head. This broke up the brain into small pieces that could be pulled from the nostril by the hook.

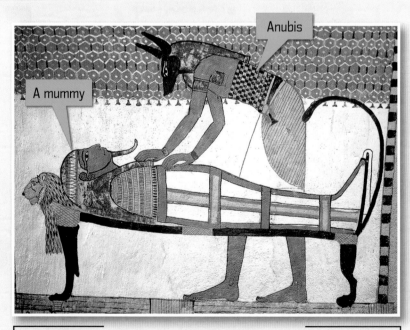

Paintings from ancient Egypt show bodies being made into mummies. Some pictures include Anubis, who was the god of embalming and the dead.

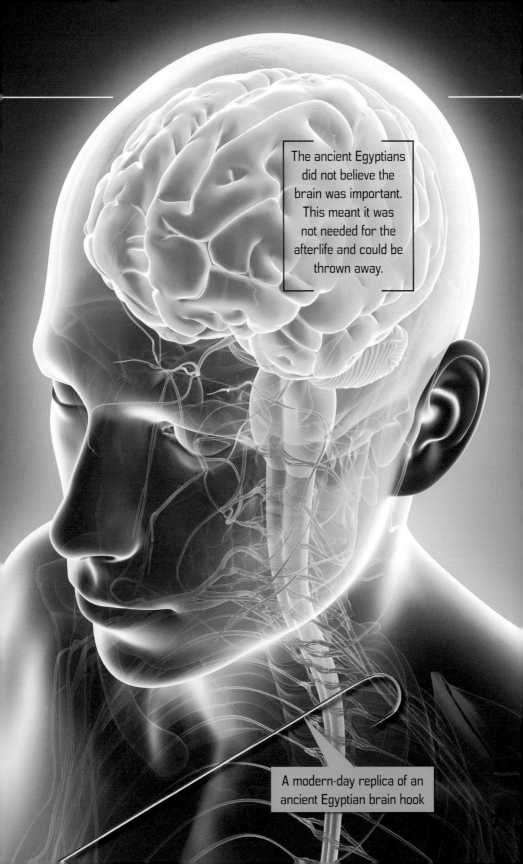

The ancient Egyptians did not believe the brain was important. This meant it was not needed for the afterlife and could be thrown away.

A modern-day replica of an ancient Egyptian brain hook

Preparing for the Afterlife

Once the embalmers had removed the brain, they began work on the chest and **abdomen**.

A small cut was made in the left side of the abdomen. Then, one of the embalmers slid his hand into the cut. Using only his sense of touch, he found the corpse's stomach and intestines. Then he pulled these organs from the body. Next, reaching farther into the body, he pulled out the lungs and liver.

All these organs were needed in the afterlife. Therefore, they were packed in a type of salt called natron salt. The salt dried out the organs and kept them from decomposing. The drying process took several weeks.

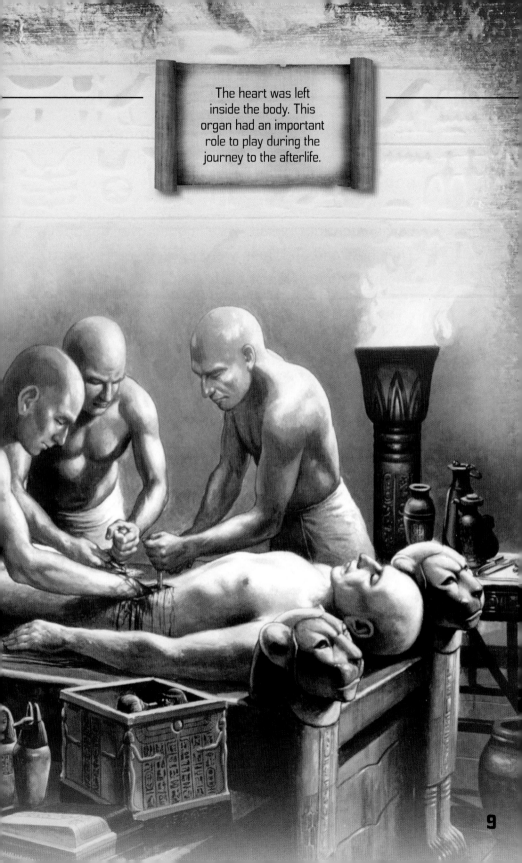

The heart was left inside the body. This organ had an important role to play during the journey to the afterlife.

Drying the Body

The next task in preparing a mummy was to dry the whole body. This was done with natron salt.

Large quantities of salt were heaped over the body. The chest and abdomen were packed with salt, too. Then the body was left to dry.

After about 35 days, any liquid in the body had dried up. The body's fat had broken down, too. The dried-out corpse was covered with dry, loose, wrinkled skin. It was also half its original weight.

After several weeks of drying, the stomach, intestines, liver, and lungs were ready, too. Each organ was carefully wrapped in **linen** cloth and placed in a jar called a canopic jar.

Natron salt was collected from the shores of lakes that contained salt water.

Salt

Mummified hand of Pharaoh Rameses IV

Many mummies have very dark skin. Scientists think that natron salt caused the skin to darken.

These canopic jars are about 3,000 years old. The jars have lids shaped like the heads of Egyptian gods. Each jar held one mummified organ.

Qebehsenuef
(falcon-headed god)
Intestines

Hapy
(baboon-headed god)
Lungs

Duamutef
(jackal-headed god)
Stomach

Imsety
(human-headed god)
Liver

Rebuilding the Body

Once the mummy's body was dry, the embalmers got to work again.

They rubbed beeswax, animal fat, and oils made from plants onto the mummy's dry skin. This softened the skin and gave the mummy a fragrant smell.

Next the embalmers rebuilt the mummy's shriveled body. They packed it with linen, sawdust, and even sandy soil. Finally, the embalmers made small cuts in the skin. Then they pushed tiny quantities of mud, sand, sawdust, and linen under the skin to smooth out any wrinkles.

Working with extreme care, the embalmers made the mummy look plump and lifelike again. The mummy's hair was styled. The embalmers even placed rings, bracelets, and a jeweled collar on the body.

Beeswax

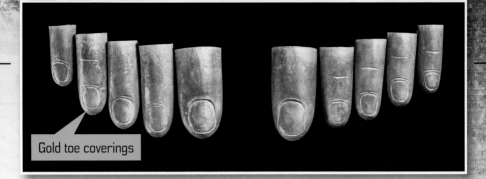

Gold toe coverings

A mummy's toes and fingernails might fall out as the skin shriveled up.
Sometimes gold coverings were put over the fingers and toes.

The mummy of Queen Nennouttaoui

A mummy's real eyes shrank during the drying process.
So new eyes made of stone or colored glass were put into
the eye sockets. This made the mummy look alive and awake.

Wrapping the Mummy

Finally, the mummy's preserved body was ready to be wrapped.

The embalmers wrapped many layers of linen around the mummy. They used sheets of linen and thin, bandage-like strips. The pieces of linen were often soaked in oils and thick, sticky **resin** from trees. Wrapping the mummy took many days.

The embalmers placed small sculptures or charms called amulets between the layers. The amulets would protect the mummy. They would also give the dead person special powers in the afterlife.

An amulet called a *wedjat* eye was placed over the cut in the mummy's abdomen. This amulet had healing powers. It would heal the cut and make the body whole again.

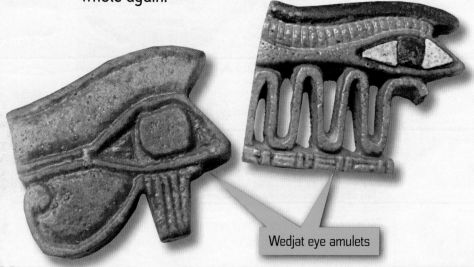

Wedjat eye amulets

Amulets

Amulets were made in many different shapes. They were made from glass, ceramic, semi-precious stones, and metals including gold.

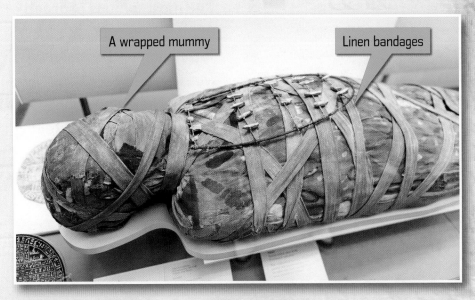

A wrapped mummy

Linen bandages

Mummy Masks and Coffins

Once the mummy was complete, a helmet-like mask was put over its face and head.

The beautiful mask gave the mummy a perfect face that would be forever young.

Finally, the mummy was placed in a coffin. In ancient Egypt, many coffins were shaped like the mummified human body. They even had a face on the lid. These mummy-shaped coffins were made of wood or stone such as granite.

The most famous pharaoh of all time is King Tutankhamun. His mummy was found inside three coffins. The outer two were made of wood decorated with gold. His innermost coffin was made of solid gold!

This mummy mask is made of plaster, linen, paper, and gold.

Inner solid gold coffin

Outer coffin made of wood

The head of Tutankhamun's gold coffin

17

Ready for the Afterlife

Inside its coffin, the mummy was taken to its burial place or tomb. The canopic jars holding the mummy's organs went, too.

As the **mourners** grieved and wept for their lost loved one, a final ceremony took place.

The ancient Egyptians believed that the spirit left the body at death. So the spirit and the body had to be reunited. The mummy mask or the face on the coffin was touched with special objects. This was called "the opening of the mouth" ceremony. This ceremony allowed the spirit to re-enter the body that had been made ready for the afterlife.

Finally, everything was done. Safe inside its coffin, the mummy was placed in an underground tomb.

This ancient Egyptian painting shows "the opening of the mouth" ceremony.

The World of the Dead

According to ancient Egyptian belief, as the mummy lay safe in its tomb, the spirit began its journey into the netherworld. This world of the dead was beneath the Earth.

The spirit traveled through the netherworld until it reached the hall of judgment. This was where the "weighing of the heart" took place.

The ancient Egyptians believed that a person's heart showed all of his or her good and bad deeds. The dead person's heart was weighed against the feather of truth. A good heart would be lighter than the feather. Its owner would be allowed to enter the afterlife.

This ancient Egyptian painting shows the "weighing of the heart" ceremony.

Anubis

Feather of truth

Heart

A heart filled with bad deeds would be heavier than the feather. This heart would be eaten by the Devourer. The bad person would never reach the afterlife, and he or she would disappear—forever!

The Devourer was a monster that was part lion, part hippo, and part crocodile.

The Devourer

Into the Afterlife

If a person passed the "weighing of the heart" test, he or she would reach the afterlife.

The ancient Egyptians had several different ideas of what the afterlife might be like. One place where a person could go was the "Field of Reeds." This beautiful place was much like the earthly world that Egyptians already knew—only better!

There were waterways for sailing boats. There were fields bursting with healthy crops. In this lush paradise, no one ever went hungry.

Once in the afterlife, the ancient Egyptians believed that a person lived on forever. In order to do this, however, he or she still needed a body. So it was essential that a person's earthly body, or mummy, was preserved and well cared for.

Caring for a Mummy

A person needed more than just a body in the afterlife. He or she also needed food and drink, and items such as clothes, jewelry, and furniture.

At the burial, family members placed these items in a person's tomb. The family then regularly brought offerings of food and drink to the tomb.

Small wooden models of food and farm animals were placed in tombs. These models gave the dead a supply of food for all eternity.

Of course, a family could not care for a mummy forever. So pictures of food, clothes, tools, and other essential objects were painted on tomb walls and on the coffin. The ancient Egyptians believed that these pictures would become real by magic. Then the dead person would have all he or she needed to live in the afterlife.

In the afterlife, a person might still have to do work. A tiny statue called a *shabti* could do the work, however, in the person's place.

Many ancient Egyptian tombs contained hundreds of shabtis.

The Book of the Dead

How do we know so much about mummies and the ancient Egyptians' beliefs about death?

Historians have studied writing and pictures in tombs and on coffins. They've also learned a lot by studying the Book of the Dead.

Ancient Egyptian tombs contained writing called hieroglyphs. Each picture sign stood for a sound, an object, or an idea.

Hieroglyphs in the tomb of Pharaoh Rameses VI

The Book of the Dead is not an actual book. It's a collection of more than 200 spells and pictures. A selection of these spells and pictures was carefully painted onto a scroll of **papyrus paper**. The scroll, or Book of the Dead, was then placed in a person's tomb. One scroll that was found is 121 feet (37 m) long!

The spells gave a person's spirit special powers and knowledge. They helped the spirit travel safely through the netherworld.

A section of papyrus from a Book of the Dead

A scroll of papyrus paper

From Cats to Queens

It wasn't only humans that were made into mummies in ancient Egypt. Millions of animals were, too. Mummified bulls, crocodiles, snakes, and fish have all been found.

Bastet was the ancient Egyptian cat goddess. Thousands of cats were mummified and given as offerings to Bastet at her temple. Many Egyptians had their pet cats, dogs, and even monkeys made into mummies. By doing this, people could take their pets with them into the afterlife.

The embalmers of ancient Egypt were masters at their craft. Thousands of years have passed, but many of the mummies they made still survive today.

Cat mummies

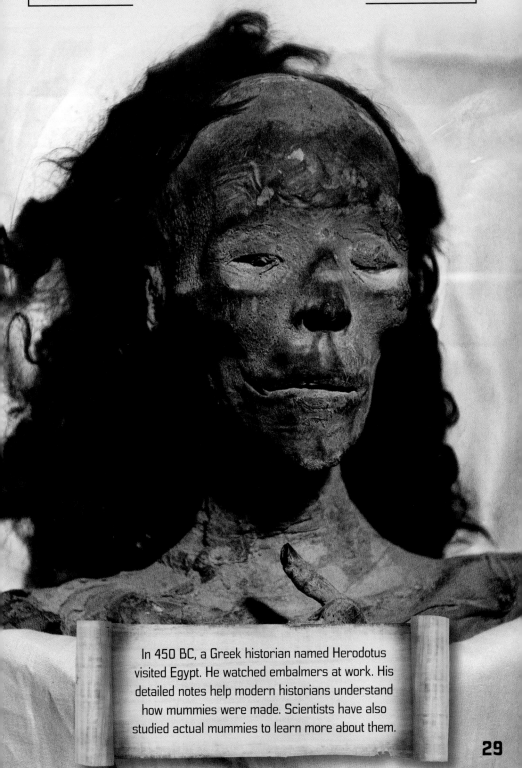

This is the mummy of Queen Tiye. She died more than 3,000 years ago in 1338 BC.

In 450 BC, a Greek historian named Herodotus visited Egypt. He watched embalmers at work. His detailed notes help modern historians understand how mummies were made. Scientists have also studied actual mummies to learn more about them.

29

Glossary

abdomen (AB-duh-min)
The part of the body that contains the stomach and other parts of the digestive system. It is also known as the belly.

afterlife (AF-tur-life)
The place where a person's spirit lives on after death.

corpse (KORPSS)
A dead human body.

embalmer (em-BAWL-mur)
A person who preserves a dead body. In ancient Egypt, embalmers made mummies.

linen (LIN-in)
A fabric made from the fibers of the flax plant.

mourner (MAWR-nur)
A person who cries and shows grief at a funeral.

mummy (MUH-mee)
The dead, and usually ancient, body of a person or animal where bones and soft tissues, such as skin, have been preserved.

organ (OR-guhn)
A body part such as the brain, heart, or stomach that has a particular job to do in the body.

papyrus paper (puh-PIE-ruhss PAY-pur)
Paper made from the fibers of the papyrus plant. These tall, reed-like plants grow on the banks of the Nile River in Egypt.

pharaoh (FAIR-oh)
A king, or ruler, of ancient Egypt.

preserved (pree-ZURVD)
Kept in its original state. For example, a preserved body will not decompose or rot.

resin (REZ-in)
A thick, sticky liquid inside the trunk and branches of some trees.

tomb (TOOM)
A room-like space where a body is buried. A tomb may be underground, in a building, or cut into rock, such as a cliff.

Index

A
afterlife, the 5, 7, 8–9,
    14, 18–19, 21, 22–23,
    24–25, 28
amulets 14–15
animal mummies 28
Anubis 6, 21

B
Book of the Dead 26–27
brains 6–7, 8

C
canopic jars 10–11, 18
Carter, Howard 17
coffins 16–17, 18, 25, 26

D
Devourer, the 21

E
embalmers 4, 6, 8–9, 12,
    14, 28–29
eyes 13, 19

G
gold 13, 15, 16–17

H
hearts 9, 20–21, 22
hieroglyphs 26

I
intestines 8, 10–11

L
linen 10, 12, 14–15, 16
liver 8, 10–11
lungs 8, 10–11

M
masks 16, 18

N
natron salt 8, 10–11
netherworld 20, 27

O
opening of the mouth
    ceremony 18–19

P
pharaohs 4, 11, 16–17,
    26

Q
queens 4–5, 13, 29

S
shabtis 25
skin 10–11, 12–13
spirits 18, 20, 27
stomach 8, 10–11

T
tombs 4, 18, 20, 24–25,
    26–27
Tutankhamun, King
    16–17

W
wedjat eyes 14
weighing of the heart,
    the 20–21, 22
wrapping a mummy
    14–15

Read More

Powell, Jillian. *The Egyptians*
(The Gruesome Truth About).
New York: Windmill Books (2011).

Putnam, James. *Mummy*
(Eyewitness). New York: Dorling
Kindersley (2009).

Learn More Online

To learn more about Egyptian mummies, go to
www.rubytuesdaybooks.com/mummy